PUBLISHED BY ZUPAKAT PRODUCTIO

C000270673

Book cover arrangement Emma François, Rob Covell and Thomas Prestø

Front cover design and Logo by: © Thomas Prestø 2008

Edited by Rob Covell

Photo courtesy of the Theatre Royal Stratford East London.

THIRD EDITION

ACKNOWLEDGEMENTS

Thank you to all those who have ever believed in me and encouraged me. Special thanks to mum who raised all seven of us with grace and humility and for encouraging and nurturing my love of reading, writing and performing.

Special mention to all my brothers and sisters who have accepted and embraced this journey that I am on. Rachel who I miss dearly and deeply, I always value the special moments we spend together. Curtis, Emma, Danny, Richie and Mari, nothing but the upmost love to you all and may you all shine in your own unique ways.

Special friends and avid supporters you are most appreciated and valued, Karen Thomas, Nick Makoha, Ebele, Sharone Monifa Knight, Sara and Peter Hazzard, Sarah and Mark Thompson and Roger Robinson.

To all my beautiful cousins, Lisa, Diane, Leanne, Clarissa, Janelle François and Auntie Lorriane, Auntie Claudine, Karina, Farelle, Cameron, Akele, Ashton.

To the next generation, Tylei, Miah, Kiah, Calvin, Chloe, Mayson and Alex and my beautiful Godson Tate.

Special mention to my wonderful cousins in Grenada, hope and love to you all.

Dawn and Karen at the Theatre Royal, Stratford East for your continued support.

Special shout out to my girl Simone, nothing but love and respect.

Special thanks to Thomas Prestø for all his hard work with the design and graphics.

Last but not least to the love of my life Rob Covell for your unconditional love and support.

Rhyme & Reason

CHILDHOOD

ONE OF SEVEN

"Rachel, Kathy,
Curtis, Emma,
Danny, Mari,
Richie."
"Yes Mum."

Home made packed lunches
Pretty hand made dresses
Made up games with cardboard boxes
Hours spent creating entire empires
Until all of us would tire
Memories of being one of seven
Are still so strong.
We were a black version of the Magnificent Seven
The Brady Bunch and the Walton's all rolled into one.
We weren't the largest family on the estate
We had the O'Conners across the road who had eight
And the O'Brians around the corner who had ten
But we were better off than those who only came in one's and two's
As there was protection in numbers,
And best of all we could play absolutely anything
Without asking a single child to join us.
British Bulldog, Knockdown Ginger
Hopscotch and Had.
"You're it, no you're it, no you're it, no you're it, MUUUUUUUUM."
Fresh bread, fried bakes, lot's of birthday cakes
Sugar water and gallons and gallons of Sarsaparilla.
We loved to watch Mary Poppins, Sound Of Music
And let's not forget Charlie And The Chocolate Factory
"I'm Charlie, I'm Charlie, no I'm Charlie."
"No you're an Umpa Lumpa."

I was second in command
Deputy leader of the troops
Rounder upper
Nose wiper
Tear stifler
Bust you up
If you touch anyone of us fighter.
Plenty of talking shoes
Put your order in early
If you want anything new
And don't forget the rules
Younger ones
Always first
First fed
And first to bed.

**"Rachel, Kathy,
Curtis, Emma,
Danny, Mari,
Richie."
"Yes Mum."**

MOTHER'S MOTHER'S LAND

Mother's mother's land
was wrapped up in childhood stories
of mango trees as tall as mountains
ripe with burnt fruit
rugby shaped and delicious
its sticky pulp shoved into salivating mouths.
Of snakes as long as rope
and as thick as muscular arms,
camouflaged waiting to scare greedy children
from their branches.
Of days spent, gallivanting
with fellow village children
playing hide and seek in sugar cane fields
which swallowed small and nimble bodies.

Mother's mother's land
sat in the multiple pots
bubbling on the stove,
filled with tender dumplings
which sunk to the bottom of caressed bowls
fished out like precious treasure.
In fruit cake, heavy with currents and raisins
moist with sprinklings of Grenadian over-proof rum
causing it to crumble flour delicate
into grateful fingers.
It was stirred into the warmth and comfort of hard food
yam, dashing, plantain,green banana and breadfruit
sitting in seven satisfied stomachs
balloon plump with fullness.

Mother's mother's land
lived in the spice box
in the middle of dark nutmeg marbles
and strips of bark
which smelt not of tree but of cinnamon,
in the brown saccharine powder
of allspice,
in the hotness of jerk seasoning
which was the catalyst
for mini fire works on the tips of tongues.
In the sharp lip tingling taste of tamarind
surprisingly sweet
and strangely bitter,
in the cool glasses of red sorrel
thirstily gulped.

Mother's mother's land,
stared out from curiously coloured pictures
which sat regally on the mantelpiece
of folk we did not recognize.
It was a faraway, exotic place
full of brown skinned inhabitants
surrounded by the bluest water
which sparkled under the heat
of the Caribbean sun.
It snuck into our English house
slipped ghost-like into our dreams
reminding us of where we really belonged.
Mother's mother's land
grew up in the house right beside us
an invisible eighth sibling.

THE TOY MONSTER

We both had a pair
of bright yellow giant sunglasses.
I broke mine.
You would not let me play with yours
so I wrested them off you
and twisted until they snapped.

We both had dolls
white skinned, blue eyed and blond haired.
I broke mine.
You would not let me play with yours
so I wrestled it from you
and twisted her neck until the head popped off.

You soon learnt to keep your toys away from me.

VICIOUS NUMBERS

Numbers scared me
Like vicious dogs.
Step-dad might stop me at any moment
And demand the time be told
On the big number clock
Which lived on the kitchen wall.
Outside my body would freeze
Like a broken down robot
Inside the panic ran around screaming
Fire, fire, fire.

For a few sweets at playtime
Michelle would always mark my maths test
Adding a few correct answers
Not too many
Just enough
So I wouldn't look stupid.
That worked very well
Until the teacher figured out
What was going on
And I was branded a cheat.

Numbers might as well have been Russian
My mind refused to hold onto them
No matter how hard I tried to concentrate
They fell through brain holes
Like slippery spaghetti.
Sometimes they'd swim around on the page
Performing perfect backstroke,
Refusing to behave.
I hate numbers.
Find them such vicious little things.

JOSIE'S GRANNY

Josie's granny came into school
To tell us what it was like to be a child
During the Second World War.
We sat cross-legged on the floor
In the big hall
She sat on a chair.
Like Josie she was tiny
She had little doll's feet
And wore shiny brown shoes.

I ate Maltesers on the way to school,
Munched on the whole packet
Did not feel well,
Saliva began to rise in my throat
Attempting to fight its way
Past my resisting tongue,
Tried to swallow it back down
But it did not work,
I was sat right in front of Josie's Granny.

The sick hit her shiny brown shoes first
Then spread across the floor.
Everyone started to scream
And scatter out of the way
Like frightened pigeons.
I clutched my stomach as the flood
Of muddy, lumpy liquid
Gushed from my mouth.
Josie's granny never did get to tell us
What it was like to be a child
During the Second World War.

ORDINARY

I was 12 when we first met
You spotted mum and me in the street.

Jumped in the back of your blue Ford
She told me you were my father.

I shyly said hello,
There were some similarities

You had teeny mouse ears just like mine
Our skin colourings matched, dark chocolate.

But I dreamt you would be taller
With a handsome movie star face

Dazzling pearly teeth
And manicured nails.

I dreamt you'd have a deep man voice,
a warm enveloping laugh.

I dreamt that when we met you would hug me
And shower me with love and long lost apologies.

But that did not happen
You were ordinary

You could have been anyone's father
I made a mental note to ask mum if she was sure.

I took sneaky looks at you
Through the rear view mirror

You smiled
I did not smile back.

BLUE IRISES AND PURPLE SUNSETS

My sister had the good hair,
long wiry coal coloured hair
which mother would twist and mould
like a pipe cleaner into any style.
Cute thin lips and a small straight nose
blessed her face,
she was beautiful.
I knew this because everyone would say so.
My brother was caramel coloured
hazel eyed with long spidery lashes
all the women would ohh and ahh
at his handsome face.

I was ugly
no one told me this, I just knew.
My hair was not pliable
and would fight back
refusing to be tamed,
mothers strong fingers would pull and tug
trying hard to manipulate the steel coils
with all the strength her arms could muster.
I sat in the middle of beauty, gloomy and broody,
my face did not inspire sun lit smiles
or the gentle caress of appreciation
my ugliness was reflected in the silence of adults.

One day mother took me aside
and whispered into young ears that black
was the most exquisite colour in the world
all the colours
melded into a single dusky entity,
that my skin carried a legacy
of struggle and triumph
and I was never to feel ashamed
of skin so enigmatic
it shone
blended with tones of
blue irises and purple sunsets.

Nostrils so spacious
they could inhale
all the enticing aromas
the earth had to offer.
Of a mouth so plump
so majestic
my words would echo loudly
whenever I spoke
and all would be forced to listen.
In her I saw myself
and because I loved her
I also learnt to love myself.

PUBERTY

Puberty hit hard
Like falling off your bike at full speed
Skidding across the ground
And taking off not one
But two layers of skin.
One breast started to grow before the other
The left one a large grape
The right a forgotten pea.

Sweat suddenly transformed
Into an annoyingly clingy friend
Following me everywhere I went,
Trickling down my forehead
Creating rivers, lakes, lagoons, seas, oceans
Of wetness, in my once dry armpits
Which I kept glued to my sides like an obedient soldier
Trying not to move them unless I really, really had to.

Five distressed trips
To the toilet
Staring, staring, staring in disbelief
At the strawberry jam stain
Which had seeped through my knickers
Before I reluctantly accepted the truth.
Within those four tiny walls
My life changed forever.

Stomach cramps,
Vicious and pulsating
Made me wrap myself up in a comforting blanket
And crawl underneath my bed
Clutching a hot water bottle,
Like a favourite teddy bear.
I would moan that I was dying
Whilst breathing in and out
In deep heavy puffs
Just as I'd seen pregnant woman
On the television do.

I was the first girl in my class
To start her period,
Once a month, head down, arm out stretched
I handed Mr Zimmerman a letter
Explaining why I could not go swimming.
Forced to stay behind,
Trapped among immature year five's,
Whilst my classmates
Splashed, screamed, laughed
And dive-bombed
BORING.

Puberty was like being first out in a game of HAD.
Puberty was like a dead arm
Delivered with a powerful punch by a mortal enemy.
Puberty was like an ice-cream headache,
Which refused to go away.
Puberty was unexpected,
Embarrassing, mortifying.
Feeling freakish I tried to ignore it,
Then I tried to send it back
To wherever it had come from,
But it rebelliously refused to leave.

WOMANHOOD

BA DAM, BA DAM, BA DAM

Thick arms
filled with the kind of strength
needed to carry heavy shopping
and crying children, sweep and sway.
Talawa legs built to stride for miles
stand sturdy and firm.
Many male and female eyes
have appreciated
the natural curve of her plump
and inviting mango calves.

She possesses a palm tree swing in her hips
gyrating to grooves
which tickle her toes
massaging clitoral muscles
causing her womb to shift
and ending in a small secret smile.
Mounds of substance and joy fill a red chiffon dress
swelling the tight material,
seams stretch to the limits of existence
but magically they hold.

Her skirt whips across her body
creating a crimson whirlwind of wonder.
She shakes off false images
of perfection
salsas self-consciousness away
banishing all past doubts
with a dip of the knees
and a flick of the head
furiously ball changing
in 4 inch fuck me heels.

Pools of dampness
gather in the pits of her arms,
unconcerned with the stubby ants
which stick out of her razor ravished skin.
She lifts palms to the goddesses and gives thanks.
Her rear has a rhythm of its own
ba dam, ba dam, ba dam, ba dam, ba dam, ba dam.
Magical mountains of mouthwatering movement
manipulatively undulate,
even as the rest of her stays silent.

She has a tooth missing
her hair is not as long, or as silky
as she would like it to be,
nor her skin as light or eyes as bright
but for now she does not give a damn.
Sycophants stand back
lizard preying,
desperate to lick off the self esteem
which seeps dew sprinkle
from her brown skin.

Tomorrow she may wake up
look in the mirror and recoil
at what stands before her
but tonight, tonight
she flies free from the stronghold of
self-loathing and criticism,
riding the back of beauty
bucking and thrusting
with the wild abandonment
of a woman who is sick and tired of hating herself.

THE DATE

Warm palms
Sit rope entwined
Sneaky sweat seeps in-between jittery fingers
No attempts made to wipe it away.
Side by side
Thighs and knees gently touch
This contact is enough
To start hearts rocket racing
And lips to pull backwards smiling.

WHITE ROSES

White roses, thrown seductively
across new made to make love sheets
classic soul tunes, wade gently through
sexually charged air.
Multi-coloured silk scarves
bind easy to capture hands
swirling kaleidoscopic images
onto wanton skin
willing minds to solidify the sin.
Candles flickering
projecting entwined images
onto silent walls witnessing,
a pliable body obeying, begging
animalistic noises calling out for release
long sort after relief.

Hips gyrating, fingers discovering
blood gorging, rushing, filling
hungered organs with longed for life.
Lips licking, hair follicles rising
eyes dominating and praising,
after dimmed light, night club kind of stripping
where each piece of clothing
is slowly peeled to reveal.....
Any residue of girl like shyness long gone
this is not the time to lie back
and think of something else,
passion over rides physical
and cultural restraints
erotic need, fills self with confidence
not ashamed to make demands.

I want gravity defying
pedestal placing
calling out my name screaming
sweat streaming
damp spot creating
night time waking to consummate
again and again.
Orgasmic swelling
constant pleasure giving
only me on your mind selfish thinking
blatant jealousy
evoking behaviour
false promises
so eager to believe in
nothing else matters only you.

RIVERS OF HOPE

Two pairs of thick lips
pressed lock tight,
brown hands,
caress, stroke and explore
memory storing for future lonely nights.
In this moment they search only for one another
blind groping in the dark
eager to please, eager to seize
this moment of opportunity.
He wipes away past hurts from her quivering body
kneading vigorously
until she butter melts in balmy hands,
opening legs which have remained closed
for longer than she cares to remember.
She releases a deep guttural groan
of both pleasure and submission
stripping away inhibitions,
up-tightness slowly peels wallpaper away
leaving only willingness behind.
Fingers, his fingers
seek and discover
turning wetness into rivers,
only when he is sure she is ready
does he enter.
He is welcome
as she spreads herself sky wide
ecstatically free from self-imposed captivity.

JOY, JOY, JOY

Head held high,
Queen of the Nile style,
as rampant fires burn where love once grew
as you peacock your new love before me.
We'd lie together
laughing, satisfied
I having cooked
your belly is heavily pregnant with good food.

I'd pretend I was fine
smile when friends asked if I was okay,
declined to talk publicly
about the break-up
shake up,
but watch humiliated
as you wrapped your octopus arms
around her.

I bumped into her all toffee coloured
big breasted and flamingo legs.
She tried to say hello but shadow hands
slowly crept around her fragile neck
squeezing traitorous breath
from uncaring lungs.
I do not really blame her
but neither do I want her in my face.

Afterwards, we would lie together
sweat, vaginal secretions and sperm
mingling with white musk incense
and chocolate scented candles.
Once we recovered
we'd start all over again
grinding against each other
hard, frantic, eager.

You told me, you wanted me
to have your child
that you could not wait for the day
when my stomach would swell
large as a watermelon full of ripe seed.
That you would be there to wipe my furrowed brow
as I pushed our creation, bloody and screaming
a mass of new flesh, bone and sinew into the light.

Found myself at church one Sunday
seeking salvation, foot stamping
clapping and chanting, "Amen, Amen, Amen."
Louder than anyone else in the congregation.
I'll never forget what the pastor said
"Don't be afraid to call on the Lord
In times of need, don't be afraid
to call on the Lord."

So when I saw the two of you together
for the first time and all I wanted to do
was call you both all the
filthy, nasty, disgusting names I knew
scratch out your lovesick eyes,
and box away the shining lighthouse bright glow
flowing effervescently from your adoring faces
with a viscous right hook

Followed by a Bruce Lee inspired round house kick
screaming that I had been betrayed.
Instead, I slammed my quivering lips shut
glued them violently together
as silent as the sea before a temper tantrum,
took a deep breath
relaxed my body, freed clenched fists
and quietly said "Joy, Joy, Joy."
over the years those three words
have continued to serve me well.

THE GODDESS WITHIN

Is forgiving and understanding
accepts her faults and imperfections.
Turns her back on self criticism and self hate
releases the memories of errant
lovers who caused stinging pain.
Forgives herself
for failing to look beyond
the depth of smooth skin
a sweet smile
slick words
and hot probing hands.
For allowing unworthy lovers
the privilege of pushing themselves inside
and consequently taking, rather than giving.
The Goddess within
lets go of rejection and betrayal
that once sat heavy in the chasm of her stomach
regurgitating negativity.

She banishes feelings of second best
and unworthiness
crushes underneath her soles
the words of hurt and hate
thrown from ugly, spitting mouths
clinging rash like to her skin.
The Goddess within
accepts her body,
the stretch marks
which run train tracks
across thighs
asymmetrical breasts,
and lumps which have appeared
in unexpected places.
Unconcerned with such trivial matters
she walks with her head high
hips swaying
imperfections on show for the world to see.

Accepts that her beauty
is in the truth of her smile
and the power of her confidence,
which on good days
stretches out before her
a ray of endless sunshine.
The Goddess within
has the ability to create life,
give breath and knit DNA
together until a living
creature crawls out from between strong thighs.
She understands her strength lies in
self-acceptance and self-love
so each morning
she flings her arms around her body
and hugs herself tight
looks in the mirror deep into her own eyes
and declares love.

KARNAPA

RIVER SALLEE JUNCTION

Muscular young men
Darkened by the strength of daily sun
Sit around the junction,
Suggestive comments thrown
At succulent girls walking by
Mango hips oscillating
Banter graciously accepted.
Small mini buses driven by fearless drivers
Vacuum packed full of commuters,
Regularly stop
Displaying names like Mello Vibes
Triumph and Hard Rine
Speedily whisking off
To Grenville, Sauteurs and St Georges.

Endlessly blue skies, amber beaches
And green vegetation
Lush with fruit and vegetables
Springs from fertile earth.
This is the land where
My ancestors walked
Where my blood
Has lived and died
For generations,
Where my mother was born and raised
Before leaving for the 'MOTHERLAND'
This is the soil
Which carries the bones of Mumma and Poppa
Mother's grandparents.

I sit underneath a large tamarind tree
Surrounded by a tribe
Of François cousins
Who either remind me of someone back home
Or remind me of my younger self.
Smooth skin
An array of beautiful brown hues
Voices strong, bell clear.
They listen intensely,
As I read Anansi stories
And recite poetry.
Their small wiry bodies pressed against mine
They stroke my hair and caress my hands
Eager to touch their new English relative.

I allow them to talk into my dictaphone,
Name, age, favourite colour, favourite food
Grenadian dialect strong.
They sing hymns
Laughingly pushing each other out of the way.
Plump brown chickens
Peck around to our left,
Three large white goats
Stomp past, herded by Goatboy
Naked to the waist
Dark skin incandescent with fresh sweat.
We sit on an old fridge someone has thrown out
Hoping that the moon continues to sleep
So we can continue to play.

THE SEED

She dances
with broad feet untouched by African soil
moving with the grace and knowledge of an ancestor.
Her hips swallowing large circular twirls
her back an arching half moon.
Within her lies knowledge, once latent
now childbirth alive.
Eyes, which have never viewed
African earth, rich with past sorrow and joys
stare into a pale world and demand respect.
Arms horizontal gathering the world towards her
leg muscles remember mislaid movements
creating intricate patterns.

Each step, each flick of the ankle
carries a message
which cannot be explained
only felt deep in the gaping aperture
left behind by clawing colourless hands
and dead hearts.
The constant throbbing of the drum
fills her body with a longing which
begins in the rippling of a liquid groin
and bursts waterfall forth
gushing and consuming,
each pulsation connects her to a past
she cannot articulate through English words.

She is a seed that has been sown
from a past unknown
but can never be lost as long as she moves
with the power of a fierce wind
devouring everything in its wake.
As long as she listens to the rhythms
born deep within curvaceous thighs
which stamp her heritage into trembling ground,
as long as she remembers that her roots
do not dig deep into European lands
but are dug endlessly into soil
rich with the blood of birth and death
rich with natural treasures and tradition,
she will always possess
an unspoken link to her heritage
even though she carries a European name
her body is instinctively conscious
of what her mind has lost,
so she dances with feet untouched by African soil
and dances with a soul that's never left.

ENGLISH GAL

Mum was right
my cousin had the same crooked gap
sitting proudly in-between her two front teeth.
The same sticky out behind
jutting out like an aeroplane wing
from the middle of her back.
We stood head to head
never having met before
but our similarities made us laugh
and hug each other tightly
as if long lost friends.

Grenada helped to rediscover
the 14-year-old child
mum left behind.
Her bare feet greedily grabbed the soil
rolling pieces of history between her toes
seeking to memorise
each piece of dirt touched.
A laugh I'd never heard before
young, girly, uninhibited
skipped out of her mouth
escaping into oven warm currants.

I jogged every morning
siphoning Grenadian air
into large and welcoming English nostrils.
Fatigued legs carried me back to the village
cheerful calls of "Good morning."
sprung from my lips greeting everyone I met
smiling, family gap on display
ignoring the amused stares
I soon became a familiar figure
embracing the calls of
"Hey English gal."

NATURAL GLORY

Thick concentric rings
regally sit on top of Nubian heads
each strand, defiant
in the face of continued
rejection and mutilation.
Each coil an antenna
creating a direct link to the heavens
channeling special blessings
which whisper affirmations
of self pride
and eternal beauty,
so all little black girls who have
naps, afros or braids
know they are special
regardless of the images of perfection
shoved down their young throats.

Their mothers are not at war with them
but eagerly accept their natural glory
lovingly wash, caress, stroke and comb
until intricate designs
passed down through generations
criss cross shiny scalps,
enhancing thick lips, wide noses
and complimenting an array of brown hues.
They learn they are worthy regardless of the length,
texture of hair or shade of skin.
Negative words bounce off sturdy backs
for they possess an armour
which enables them to see and feel beauty
where many only see and feel ugly
causing them to stride around
with super heroine confidence.

They walk as tall and proud as warriors
and do not care if their locks
fail to blow in the wind
nor do they feel inadequate when white girls
or straight haired sisters preen by.
They do not spend hours
dying, straightening, transforming
placing jumpers or towels on heads
so they too can flick endlessly.
They do not grow into women who do not allow men
to massage their aching scalps, sensually
missing out on important, male, female intimacy.
They are not the kind of women
who try and maintain exact sexual positions
which do not cause weaves
or wigs to be disturbed.

Neither are they afraid of rain
but graciously welcome
the cool liquid which sustains life.
Thick concentric rings
regally sit on top of grown Nubian heads
each strand
defiant in the face
of continued rejection and mutilation.
These women banish
false images of attraction
shoved down the throats
of daughters, nieces, aunts,
mothers and grandmothers
turn their back on Eurocentric ideals
which prove wholeheartedly unattainable
and wholeheartedly accept themselves.

DHURUPUTJPI

Blue-black skin darkened by the sun
Scrawny toothpick legs, deceptively strong
Hair ranging from luxuriantly woolly Afros
To arrow straight tresses,
Frames their faces.
Fierce heat beats onto brown skin
Only familiar with English temperatures
So the hottest part of the day
Is spent hiding underneath a large tree
Trying to move as little as possible.

A lone dingo has taken a liking to the camp
Scrawny and pale
It skulks around the edges
Vulture scavenging for discarded scraps.
My morning run is interrupted
By the padding of its feet
As it follows closely behind
Heart beats fast, but two large sticks
And an array of loud strange noises
Soon scares it away.

Follow the women as they pick plants
Pulling, tugging,
Talking, laughing
Until limp fibres lay in their hands
Later they will be soaked in boiling water
To create dye for mats and baskets.
They slap the water to ward off crocodiles
Beckon me to join them
But fear caused by watching too many
Wild life documentaries will not allow me.

Nights are spent
Crouched around a blazing campfire,
Ignoring the heat
Coats are pulled up
covering ears and fingers
warding off aggressive mosquitoes
Which ruthlessly attack
Flames keep them away.
Songs sung and stories weaved
Float away into engulfing darkness.

A tiny tent is home for two weeks
The silence at night times is oppressive
No city lights, no noise pollution
Just thoughts.
Too scared to make my way to the toilet,
Which is a wooden hut 50 yards away
Spend hours crossing my legs
Praying for sunrise.
On my last night they named me Karnapa
The woman who travels.

ADVERSITY

GUILT

Everyday I watch as you struggle
To rise out of a simple chair.
Crutches are your second pair of legs
Causing your back to hunch,

The metallic limbs stretch before you
Producing an alien shuffle.
I hold you as muscles
Which used to support unaided, give way.

A beetle stuck the wrong way around
You lay vulnerable and helpless
I grip you with strength
I do not know I possess.

Somehow we scramble up.
I run everyday
Forcing wind into my lungs
Eager to flee the feebleness of your body

Pounding into the ground
With as much force as I can muster,
Driving guilty legs forward
Desperate to take steps for you.

On bad days I scream my frustration into the trees
Which do not judge, criticize
Or try to comfort
But silently absorb the pain.

WEIGHTY ISSUES

Offending rolls
are pulled and tugged
until they ache
like manipulated dough.
Moments in the mirror
spent criticising
berating and hating.
Denial makes my cravings worse
supermarket trips
turn into torment
the bakery section
calls my name
enticing me to buy, buy, buy
so later I can lick, kiss and satisfy
my craving for sugar.

Either I am in the throes of losing
or the throes of gaining.
Hours spent in the gym
sweating like a mad woman
trying to ignore the stick insects
training by my side
taunt mid-sections on display
like lean chicken
tiny breasts bouncing
with each languid step.
I turn up the speed and run faster
arms pumping, legs flying
as if I am running an Olympic 100 metres
I leave the skinny girls behind
their meagre frames cannot keep up.

I hide a stomach
filled with blubber
which I fight to control
secret big girl briefs are a Godsend.
Arms flap bat fashion in the wind
and thighs fail to look decent
even in the blackest of trousers.
Hips no longer appear smooth in a tight fitting dress
but appear porridge lumpy.
I try to find the Goddess within
and love all of me regardless of what the scales say.
Some days I feel voluptuous and sexy
others I try to dampen rising panic
when nothing in my wardrobe fit's
and I struggle to look decent.

HURT

Hurts to breathe
Unseen pressure
Crushes a quivering chest
Stomach tied into impossible knots,
Throat endlessly dry
No amount of fluid
Can quench this thirst.
Nights spent alone
Adrift
Vulnerability clings to tingling skin
Aching to feel a vanishing caress,
Do not wish to forget the firm touch of welcome lips
Or the gentle stroke of enquiring hands,
Fearful that the memories
Implanted into my body
Fingertip by fingertip
Will dissipate forever.

HEATHROW

Rough hands with no respect
Grab and grope her breasts
With the franticness of a blind man
Searching for a diamond.
Surprised, she steps back
But is told to once again raise her arms,
Feeling as if she has no other choice
She obediently does as commanded.
Stands in the shape of a cross, legs spread
Humiliation creeps slowly up her neck into her face
Exploding in her mind,
Spectators watch
Immediately judging.

Her dark skin
Acts like a stain on the soul,
Supposedly revealing her true nature
To some who seem to possess special powers,
So that before she has opened her mouth
Or made any moves
That may indicate suspicion
They are certain she is guilty.
Her brownness
Which covers their identical bones
Is viewed as a living carpet of shame
The only excuse needed to
Discriminate and segregate.

She stands perfectly still
The belt of her trousers hangs open
Pale hands feel inside her briefs
Curving around her buttocks searching.
Her face pinched,
Teeth violently clenched
A slight twitch attacks strong fingers
But they remain silent.
Raging rivers build behind fast blinking eyes
But the dam holds
Refusing to release the deluge of emotion.
A final pat down of her crutch
And the assault is over.

Long strides sweep away a trembling body
Her throat is tight
Unable to release a single word.
But her mind incubates
A volcano filled with furious lava
Afraid she will breathe fire,
And incinerate everything which surrounds
Thick lips remain clamped shut.
The stain sits heavily on her back
It will not wash away
But shall transform itself into an invisible scar
Ripping huge chunks from the self-confidence
She has fought so hard to gain.

KIN

Marched next to mothers with absent sons
silent tears streamed along their distressed faces

Leaving tracks, which could only hint
At the trauma experienced.

I stood alone a stranger
But not a stranger to police violence

Thought back to the 24-year-old woman
Whose breath had almost stopped

To the knees rammed aggressively into a prone spine
To rough hands forcing her head into the rancid van floor.

Women screamed during the speeches
Wailing for lost sons who would never return.

Beginning in the park where the young
Aboriginal boy's life ended

We marched the streets of Redfern
Surrounded by swaying flags

Held tightly within clenched fists
Black for beautiful skin

Red for the earth and love of the land
Yellow the life giver.

Tales of vacant wombs
Too old to be replenished shattered fragile nerves

My own screams of terror and fear haunted me,
Put my hands over my ears

So I would not hear my past self
Gasping for vanishing breath

One step, two-step, three steps
I willed my feet to continue,

The sun shone
Yet shadows reigned,

Home was far, but I stood with distant kin
United by the colour of abused and battered skin.

Thought of my own mother
Who had almost lost a child

On a West London street
Ten thousand, five hundred miles away.

A woman reached out and embraced me
We cried, soaking up each other's grief

Sat on hot tarmac
Hip to hip, shoulder to shoulder

Swapped stories
And called each other sister.

Kat François

Kat Francois is a performance poet, playwright, director, actor, comedian, and workshop facilitator. She was the first person to win a televised poetry slam in the UK, on BBC3 in 2004, and a year later went on to win the World Slam Poetry Championships in Rotterdam. She has performed nationally and internationally, including Germany, Norway, Sweden, Rome, Eire, The Netherlands, Austria, Italy, Australia, USA and Canada.

A well-known performance poet on the London poetry scene, Kat has been hosting a monthly poetry and music event, Word4Word, for 13 years at Theatre Royal Stratford East. Kat creates a positive and welcoming space for poets and musicians to share their work attracting both new and established artists, all interspersed with her comedic hosting.

As a playwright, Kat has written and performed two solo plays, SEVEN TIMES ME, RAISING LAZARUS, and two comedy shows, KAT'S GOT YOUR TONGUE and THE KAT FRANCOIS COMEDY SHOW, which received a 5 star review at the Camden Fringe Festival.

She has worked with young people for many years, as a youth worker, PHSE Facilitator, also teaching, dance, drama, poetry and performance skills.

Kat is an established director of youth theatre, devising plays for theatres including Theatre Royal Stratford East, Roundhouse Camden, Lyric Theatre Hammersmith, as well as performances at Arcola Theatre, and Camp Bestival.

Kat also works with young poets at Theatre Royal Stratford East, every Monday evening, where they work on their performance and writing skills and put on regular performances.

Kat has performed numerous times on BBC radio and television including BLUE PETER and the BIG POETRY SLAM, an educational television programme that is still being repeated. Kat was also interviewed live on BBC breakfast television to mark the passing of Maya Angelou where she performed the famous poem, "STILL I RISE."

Kat has released a spoken word CD entitled BLESSED BY WORDS and is published in a number of poetry magazines and anthologies. Her first written collection of poetry, RHYME AND REASON, was published in February 2008 and is now in its third edition. She is currently working on her second collection.

At present she is working on her solo play Raising Lazarus, which explores the experiences of Caribbean soldiers during the First World War. Raising Lazarus has been shown at Nottingham Play House, Rich Mix London, Decibel Manchester, The Hawth Crawley, Theatre Royal Stratford East, London and the Camden Fringe Festival.

Raising Lazarus has also been performed in Canada and will continue to tour internationally.

For more information visit www.katfrancois.com